GINGERBREAD
FUNNIES

GINGERBREAD
FUNNIES
ADAM SCHEFF

GIBBS SMITH
TO ENRICH AND INSPIRE HUMANKIND

To my family

14 13 12 11 10   5 4 3 2 1

Text © 2010 Adam Scheff
Illustrations © 2010 Adam Scheff

Published by
Gibbs Smith
P.O. Box 667
Layton, Utah 84041

1.800.835.4993 orders
www.gibbs-smith.com

Designed by Black Eye Design, Inc.
Printed and bound in Hong Kong
Gibbs Smith books are printed on paper produced from sustainable
PEFC-certified forest/controlled wood source.
Learn more at: www.pefc.org

Library of Congress Control Number: 2010922351
ISBN 13: 978-1-4236-1686-3
ISBN 10: 1-4236-1686-3

Julius Ginger

Vertigo Gingerbread Man

The Gingerbread Shop Teacher

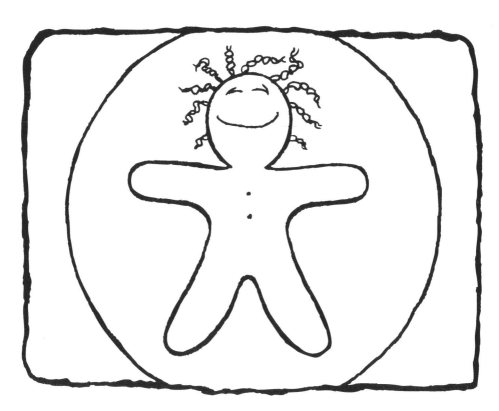

Gingerbread Rastaman

Quicksand Gingerbread Man

Mr. G

Gingerbread Proctologist

Injuredbread Man

Constipated Gingerbread Man

Too Much Bran Man

Phantom of the Cookie Jar

Gingerbread Puberty

Gingerbread Mad Men

Odor Eaters Gingerbread Man

Gingerbread Mob Informer

Gingerbread Man with a Migraine

Gingerbread Euro-woman

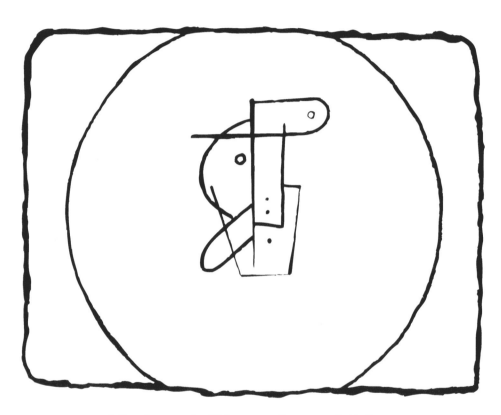

Abstract Gingerbread Man

Bad Tattoo Gingerbread Man

Ginger and Mary Ann

Lockjaw Gingerbread Man

Gingerbread Lincoln

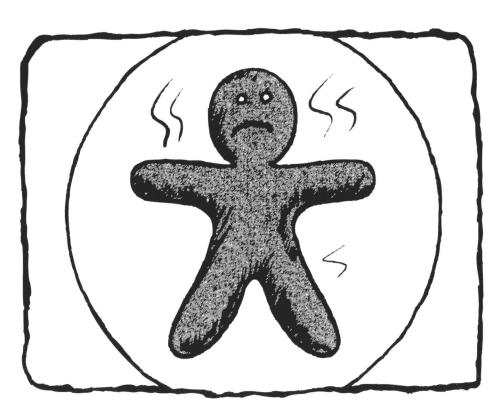

Gingerbread Joan of Arc

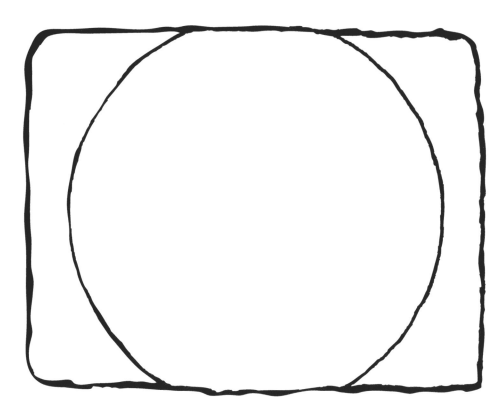

M.I.A. Gingerbread Man

Brain Damaged Gingerbread Man

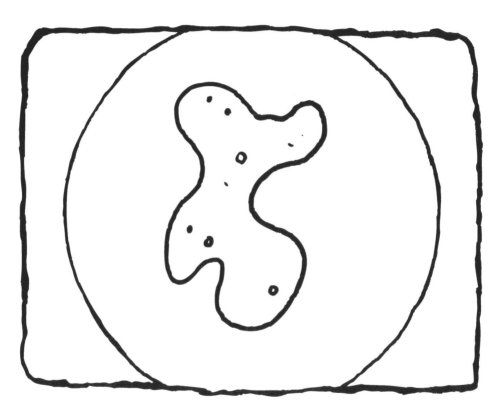

Ginger Germ

Gingerbread Man Who Swallowed a Fly

Disco-bread Man

Gingeration X

Gingerbread Cellulite

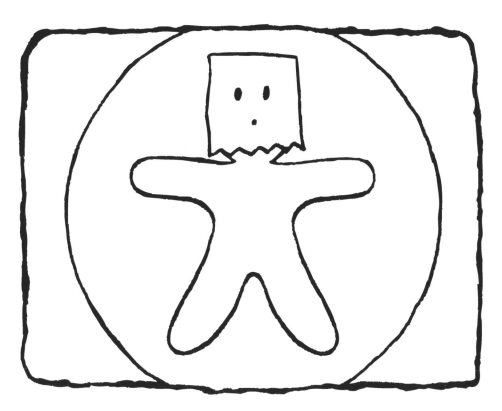

The Unknown Gingerbread Man

No Bread Man

Gingerbread and Water Man

Gingerbread Birth Control

Dandruff Man

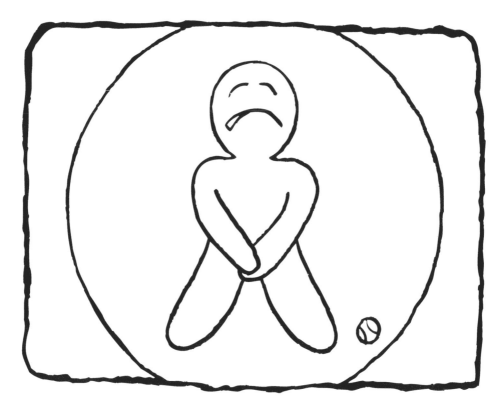

Soprano Gingerbread Man

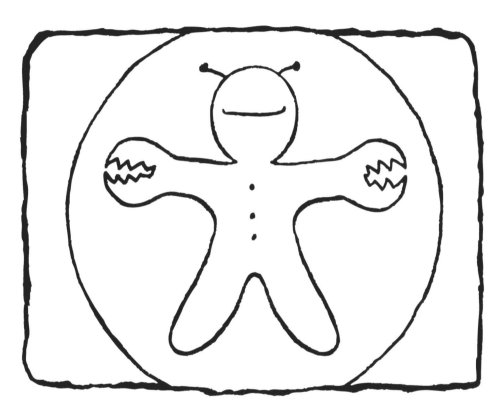

Gingerbread Lobster Boy

Carpal Tunnel Syndrome Man

Gingerbread Nag

Gingerbread Protester

Allergic to Ginger Gingerbread Man

Swiss Army Gingerbread

Gingerbread Tries to Do Jumping Jacks

Gingerbread Organ Donor

Exotic Gingerbread Dancer

Gingerbread Fan

Gingerbread Gothic

Ginger the Hutt

Incognito Gingerbread Man

Wonderbread Woman

Gingerettes

Yoga Man

Bingerbread Man

Gingerbread Love Handles

Alien Probed Man

Addicted to Sprinkles Man

Fred and Ginger

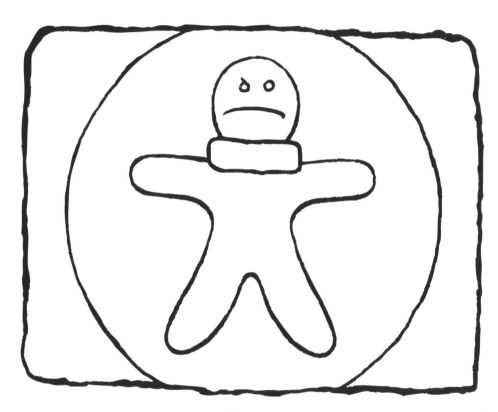

Whiplash Man

Gingerdead Man